Know Your Numbers

Lots of Ladybugs!

Counting by Fives

Special thanks to our advisers for their expertise:

Stuart Farm, M.Ed., Mathematics Lecturer
University of North Dakota, Grand Forks

Susan Kesselring, M.A., Literacy Educator
Rosemount-Apple Valley-Eagan (Minnesota) School District

by Michael Dahl illustrated by Todd Ouren

PICTURE WINDOW BOOKS
Minneapolis, Minnesota

Managing Editor: Catherine Neitge
Creative Director: Terri Foley
Art Director: Keith Griffin
Editor: Christianne Jones
Designer: Todd Ouren
Page production: Picture Window Books
The illustrations in this book were prepared digitally.

Picture Window Books
1710 Roe Crest Drive
North Mankato, MN 56003
www.capstonepub.com

Library of Congress Cataloging-in-Publication Data
Dahl, Michael.
Lots of ladybugs! : counting by fives / written by Michael Dahl ; illustrated by Todd Ouren.
p. cm. — (Know your numbers)
ISBN-13: 978-1-4048-0944-4 (hardcover)
ISBN-13: 978-1-4048-1118-8 (paperback)
1. Counting—Juvenile literature. 2. Multiplication—Juvenile literature. 3. Ladybugs—Juvenile literature. I. Ouren, Todd, ill. II. Title.

QA113.D337 2005
513.2'11—dc22 2004019003

Printed in the United States 5188

Look at all the ladybugs!

A lazy ladybug lounges on a leaf.
FIVE black spots on her red, red shell.

5

Careful ladybugs climb a curly stem.

5

10

TEN black spots on their red, red shells.

Busy ladybugs buzz above a bush.
FIFTEEN black spots
on their red, red shells.

15

Restless ladybugs race across the roses.

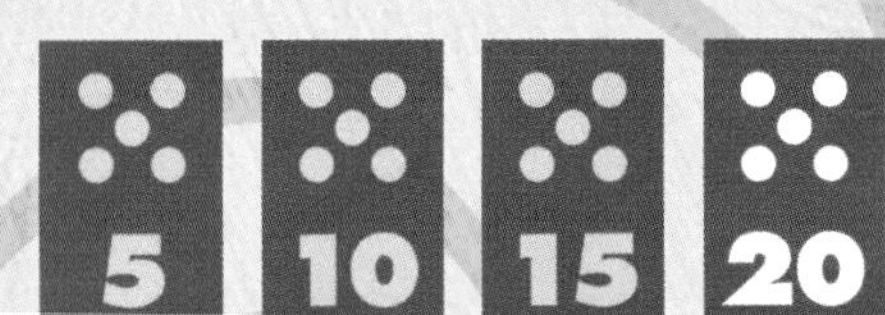

TWENTY black spots
on their red, red shells.

Hungry ladybugs hunt in the high grass.

TWENTY-FIVE black spots
on their red, red shells.

Curious ladybugs creep by a caterpillar.

5 10 15 20 25 30

THIRTY black spots
on their red, red shells.

Look-alike ladybugs line up on a log.

THIRTY-FIVE black spots
on their red, red shells.

Proud ladybugs parade upon potatoes.

FORTY black spots
on their red, red shells.

5 10 15 20 25 30 35 40 45

Friendly ladybugs feel like
feathers on my fingers.

FORTY-FIVE black spots
on their red, red shells.

Loads of ladybugs live on our lot!

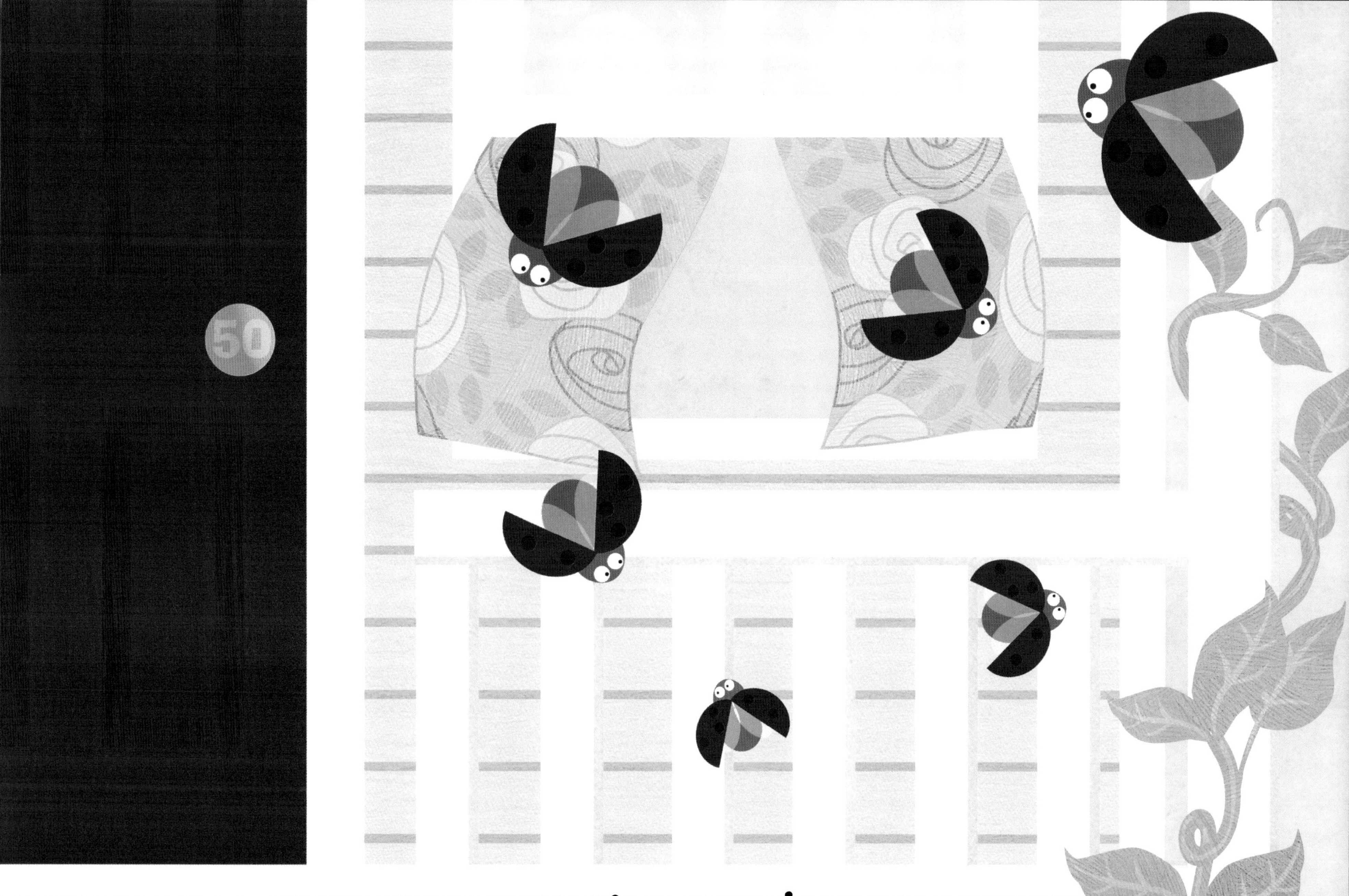

FIFTY black spots
on their red, red shells.

Fun Facts

- Ladybugs are usually red or orange. But they can also be red, yellow, gray, black, blue, or pink.
- Ladybugs like it hot! They won't fly if the temperature is below 55 F (13 C).
- Ladybugs are also called ladybirds or lady beetles.
- As a ladybug grows older, the spots on its back will fade.
- When a ladybug is in danger, it may "play dead" to fool an enemy.

On the Web

FactHound offers a safe, fun way to find Web sites related to this book. All of the sites on FactHound have been researched by our staff.

1. Visit *www.facthound.com*
2. Type in this special code: 1404809449
3. Click on the FETCH IT button.

Your trusty FactHound will fetch the best Web sites for you!

Find the Numbers

Now you have finished reading the story, but a surprise still awaits you. Hidden in each picture is a multiple of 5 from 5 to 50. Can you find them all?

5–on the leaf to the right of the ladybug

10–on the curl of the stem on the left page

15–in the middle of the bottom flower on the right page

20–in the middle of the top flower on the right page

25–the legs of the bug on the right page

30–on the caterpillar's middle spot

35–on the leaf between the bugs on the left page

40–on the rim of the bowl on the right page

45–between the boy's fingers

50–on the doorknob

Look for all of the books in the Know Your Numbers series:

Downhill Fun
A Counting Book About Winter

Eggs and Legs
Counting By Twos

Footprints in the Snow
Counting By Twos

From the Garden
A Counting Book About Growing Food

Hands Down
Counting By Fives

Lots of Ladybugs!
Counting By Fives

On the Launch Pad
A Counting Book About Rockets

One Big Building
A Counting Book About Construction

One Checkered Flag
A Counting Book About Racing

One Giant Splash
A Counting Book About the Ocean

Pie for Piglets
Counting By Twos

Starry Arms
Counting By Fives